DIRTY MARTINI

Natalie Shaw has been described as 'wonderfully bananas' by the TLS. Her pamphlet *Oh be quiet* is published by Against the Grain press. She has been commended in the National Poetry Competition and shortlisted in the Bridport prize. Her poems can be found in many journals and anthologies, including Bloodaxe's *Staying Human*.

ISBN: 978-1-915079-57-2

Cover designed by Aaron Kent

Edited & Typeset by Aaron Kent

Broken Sleep Books Ltd   Broken Sleep Books Ltd
Rhydwen   Fair View
Talgarreg   St Georges Road
Ceredigion   Cornwall
SA44 4HB   PL26 7YH

Dirty Martini

Natalie Shaw

Also by Natalie Shaw

Oh Be Quiet   (Against the Grain, 2020)

CONTENTS

Poached Trout

Little fish
Delicious fish
delicious fish
      how I love you little fish

How you shine
in my palm
      happy fish
            you can't breathe
      happy fish

There in the dark
      a flicker

Pig in Space

ur so alone out here
maybe it's all in ur head
BE VERY AFRAID!!!!
if u were mad how wud u kno
like u wud have a clue
I can't hear u no one can
cry all u like
are u trying to call me?
lol

Self-Portrait as Pink Grapefruit Segment

Aha it me
Take up your serrated spoon
Cast off this kidskin pith
(Am vegan tho)
I am so fucking complicated
How to describe my endocarp
My juicy vesicles
My interfering furanocoumarins?
Bergamottin this.

Baby, have you have you?

I have been to the moon and back   no really
you can go too   if you like   I took supplies
the moon was far away but real
in a different way to now   now I am back
here   it's hard to remember   how movement was heavy but
very fine and light simultaneously *careful now*   there was
water too   all over the carpet   the washing machine broke
it was full of towels   the silent fairground   on the moon
such pretty lights   I saw all of this   in the dark
I did   and more   we were washing the towels
it all happened   there on the moon   *and also*

Gingerbread House

Everything in the icehouse
can be eaten
Girl: (licks bricks)
  -    - - - -
Girl: Ah my tongue

(there's no answer
in the icehouse)

Girl: Mum I'm made
Of ice now mum
I think I'm
an ice girl

(no one is listening
in the icehouse)

(no one)

Girl: (through the ice)
Girl: (says nothing)

Through the pink bricks

Girl: (thinks) That witchy woman!

Hundreds of bricks
And a ladder down

It is terrible, terrible

Party for Hares

The hares are waxing again.
Their multiple long ears silhouette into one
hard-to-parse shape against the wall.

It is my fault. It is because
I have left the door open, again.
They have always found their way in.

Now there are so many hares I can barely breathe.
They have a purpose unrelated to fun.
I am surrounded and it's hard to breathe.

The hares are mingling and the crisps have run out.
They are treading crisp shards into the carpet.
They are making a mess of everything!

The hares are busy with their own thing.
They will break everything.
They have their own business in mind.

Crow in HMP Downview

Crow cocks her eye.
It's time

Says crow,
To go.

Outside, we hear
Crow's wings

Hit brick.
Hit brick.

Crow caws,
Crow flies

Nowhere.
Fanatic crow

Says no:
See how

I go.

Vegetable Love

We were green and salad-like,
Spring oniony and spiky.
We waited with our crispy hearts,
Desiring only slicing.

Dirty Martini

We outgrew custard
We hollered for sequins
Like this: SEQUINS NOW
Not enough

We were terrific in tulle
Our lorgnettes were so gorgeous

Whip our cream
PAVLOVA
Beat our meringue
GLOSSY PEAKS
Bring our spoon
BEGONE

What spoiled us?
Oh you, you did, it was you
All along.
We were blameless
In the ballroom

WHERE IS OUR FIZZ
BRING US OUR FIZZ

Trickster at Acton Central

I am the bicycle under the water
I am the gold lights that flicker and bead
I am the dark fish swimming, swimming
I am the nematode,
swallow me whole

I am the thread snaking through fabric
I am the bus and the shaking palm
I am the black box which houses the answer
I am the labyrinth,
follow me down

I am the mirror that shunts away lamplight
I am the silver that holds you just so
I am the shout in your dream that stays silent
I am the echo
narrow my mouth

I am the dark road that goes round forever
I am the lightlessness all through the park
I am the bicycle pedalling, pedalling
I am the tree nymph
borrow my crown

I am the quiet thing waiting to meet you
I am the blood that knocks in your sockets
I am the minutes you made yourself quiet for
I am the woman
furrow her through

I am the blackness skewing inside you
I am the snakes pushing through skin
I am the night time held down in the gravel
I am the statue
I am the stone

Rough Rabbit

Waterloo, 2007

I
Rabbit under the arches of the S Mex building
At the end of a long line of rabbits in sleeping bags

Rabbit who knows what it once was
Now it was

> down on its luck
> a bit mad
> most likely alcoholic

Other rabbits become vulnerably housed
Rabbit was once

> housed, I guess

II
Let's have a bit of fun
Let's keep ourselves warm eh

Rabbit went WHOOSH when I dropped the match
My own crap rabbit firework
Burn rabbit burn
What is the point of you now

Walk in the Park

There's a bear over there   say hello   I'd like to
Hey human   yes bear   how much bear
is possible   once, at a picnic   *enough*
is enough   little girl   how much bear
being eaten   a real possibility   too much
oh over there   tiny fallings   what we all saw
a talking bear   there on the screen   why
aren't you blue   hello sky   what can you see
from the sky   how much bear   not enough
we have to keep eating   or not

Caribou

That night she fell asleep
in the ice house
It is the shape of an egg

She fell asleep in the ice house

The ice creaks
The cold air blankets her up

As she slept she missed
Michaelmas, Play and Election terms,
cycle after cycle; her birthdays; she was
no longer included
in pictures or on invitations.
Her notifications
Built up. *The ice*

melts and is replenished

from the frozen lake outside
several times

As she woke, her head was heavy
Her antlers pushed through the shell

as she stretched,
several times.

She stepped back outside,

some different lightness
about her.

Party Invitation with Knife

The invite read
Things'd be better
If you were dead.

Disagree? Come
To my knife fight.
It'll be fun
For me.

Baba Yaga Learns not to Drown

Using my fingernail, I sliced
A neat seam down my ribcage.

Opening the seam, I fitted myself
with tiny silk pockets in beautiful colours,

a school of Golden Cloud Mountain minnows,
or the branches of a tree lighting

into blossom.
I whispered air into their little lungs

and sang my favourite lullabies to soothe them,
before I sewed the seam back up

neat as a leaf.
Each time under the water

I felt the smooth silk open under my fingers
blossoming pocket by pocket.

Mezuzah

This way one thing
That way another

It is a literal fairyland
To be with you

See how the light falls
Like fine rain from the trees

Step with me
We're dancing now

Across the threshold
Palm to palm

ACKNOWLEDGEMENTS

Previous versions of some of these poems have been published by *Tentacular, Perverse, The Rialto, Magma* and *Butcher's Dog.*

Lay out your unrest

Lightning Source UK Ltd.
Milton Keynes UK
UKHW041934170123
415517UK00006B/862